Delightful Handwriting
Teacher Book

by
Lanaya Gore

Delightful Handwriting Teacher Book
Text © 2011, Lanaya Gore

Cover Design: John Shafer
Cover Art: Jessie Willcox Smith

ISBN 978-1-61634-136-7 (printed book)
ISBN 978-1-61634-137-4 (e-book)

Published and printed by
Simply Charlotte Mason, LLC
P. O. Box 892
Grayson, Georgia 30017-0892

SimplyCharlotteMason.com

Contents

Introduction

Children work so hard at their young age to learn some of the very basics of education: reading and writing. Charlotte Mason had a unique philosophy which strove to teach children in a natural, simple, and interesting way. This handwriting manual and child's copybook will help your child learn to write according to Charlotte Mason principles.

You can first read what Charlotte said about copywork. The next section is the teacher instruction on how to form capital and lowercase letters. Throughout the lessons will be quotes and reminders on how to apply Charlotte's principles to teach handwriting.

Two different font choices are offered, D'Nealian and Zaner Bloser, and this instruction book is all you need to teach either choice.

When possible, words from *Delightful Reading* were chosen with which your child could practice writing in his copybook. This has the benefit of extra reading review if *Delightful Reading* is your choice for reading instruction. Words from the poem *Rain* are used during the capital letter lessons. And words from *The Dogs and the Fox* and Proverbs are used during the lowercase letter lessons. At the very end of the lessons, all three selections are written out in large print for your child to copy for practice. Extra lined pages are also included for the teacher's own writing practice ideas.

What a privilege to be able to teach your child such a useful skill as writing! Enjoy the journey together!

Part 1

Charlotte Mason's Own Words

Charlotte Mason on Teaching Handwriting

1. A beautiful style of handwriting helps cultivate your child's taste for beauty. Do not allow vulgar handwriting.

"Some years ago I heard of a lady who was elaborating, by means of the study of old Italian and other manuscripts, a 'system of beautiful handwriting' which could be taught to children. I waited patiently, though not without some urgency, for the production of this new kind of 'copy-book.' The need for such an effort was very great, for the distinctly commonplace writing taught from existing copy-books, however painstaking and legible, cannot but have a rather vulgarising effect both on the writer and the reader of such manuscript. At last the lady, Mrs Robert Bridges, has succeeded in her tedious and difficult undertaking, and this book for teachers will enable them to teach their pupils a style of writing which is pleasant to acquire because it is beautiful to behold. It is surprising how quickly young children, even those already confirmed in 'ugly' writing, take to this 'new handwriting' " (Vol. 1, pp. 235, 236).

A sample of Mrs. Bridges' new handwriting.

Vulgar means "lacking refinement, culture, or taste."

2. A beautiful model of the letters or words and interesting content should keep copywork lessons interesting and pleasant.

"I should say that variety and beauty of form are attractive, even to little children, and that the attempt to create something which interests them, cheers and crowns their stupendous efforts with a pleasure that cannot be looked for in the task of copying monotonous shapes" (Vol. 1, p. 237).

"A sense of beauty in their writing and in the lines they copy should carry them over this stage of their work with pleasure" (Vol. 1, p. 239).

3. Your child should continue writing a medium size until he can make his letters with ease.

" 'Text-hand,' the medium size, should be continued until he makes the letters with ease" (Vol. 1, p. 235).

4. Do not hurry your child into writing small; it can instigate bad habits.

"One word more; do not hurry the child into 'small hand'; . . . . It is much easier for the child to get into an irregular scribble by way of 'small-hand,' than to get out of it again. In this, as in everything else, the care of the educator must be given, not only to the formation of good, but to the prevention of bad habits" (Vol. 1, p. 235).

5. Do not require your child to copy elaborate or ornamental writing.

"If he write in books with copperplate headlines (which are, on the whole, to be eschewed), discrimination should be exercised in the choice of these; in many of them the writing is atrocious, and the letters are adorned with flourishes which

"Variety and beauty of form are attractive, even to little children."

Notes

An example of an elaborate heading and copperplate handwriting.

"In this, as in everything else, the care of the educator must be given, not only to the formation of good, but to the prevention of bad habits."

increase the pupil's labour but by no means improve his style" (Vol. 1, p. 235).

6. Make sure your child's work surface is well lit and that his body is not casting a shadow across his work.

"For the writing position children should sit so that light reaches them from the left" (Vol. 1, p. 239).

7. The desk or table should be at a comfortable height for your child.

"Desk or table should be at a comfortable height" (Vol. 1, p. 239).

8. Teach your child to hold a pencil or pen correctly.

"It would be a great gain if children were taught from the first to hold the pen between the first and second fingers, steadying it with the thumb. This position avoids the uncomfortable strain on the muscles produced by the usual way of holding a pen—a strain which causes writer's cramp in later days when there is much writing to be done. The pen should be held in a comfortable position, rather near the point, fingers and thumb somewhat bent, and the hand resting on the paper. The writer should also be allowed to support himself with the left hand on the paper, and should write in an easy position, with bent head but not with stooping figure" (Vol. 1, p. 239).

9. Teach a young child to write only if he is interested in it.

"A child will have taught himself to paint, paste, cut paper, knit, weave, hammer and saw, make lovely things in clay and sand, build castles with his bricks; possibly, too, will have taught himself to read, write, and do sums, besides acquiring no end of knowledge and notions about the world he lives in, by the time he is six or seven. What I contend for is that he shall do these things because he chooses (provided that the standard of perfection in his small works be kept before him)" (Vol. 1, pp. 193, 194).

10. Beginning writing lessons require your child to learn how to control his hand and make it draw what he sees in his mind's eye.

"A child must first learn to control his hand and constrain it to obey his eye" (Vol. 1, p. 236).

11. Practice letters first on the chalkboard or whiteboard, later with pencil on paper, then with pen and ink.

"In all writing lessons, free use should be made of the blackboard by both teacher and children by way of model and practice" (Vol. 1, p. 239).

"At this stage the chalk and blackboard are better than pen and paper, as it is well that the child should rub out and rub out until his own eye is satisfied with the word or letter he has written" (Vol. 1, p. 234).

"The method of using Mrs Bridges' *Handwriting*, which we find most effectual, is to practise each form on the blackboard from the plate, and later to use pencil, and still later pen and ink" (Vol. 1, p. 237).

12. Beginning writing lessons should be short, not more than five or ten minutes.

"Let the writing lesson be short; it should not last more than five or ten minutes" (Vol. 1, p. 233).

13. Encourage your child to accomplish something perfectly in every writing lesson, whether a stroke or a letter. Avoid forming the habit of careless work.

"I can only offer a few hints on the teaching of *writing*, though much might be said. First, let the child accomplish something perfectly in every lesson—a stroke, a pothook, a letter. . . . Ease in writing comes by practice; but that must be secured later. In the meantime, the thing to be avoided is the habit of careless work— humpy *m*'s, angular *o*'s" (Vol. 1, pp. 233, 234).

" 'Throw perfection into all you do' is a counsel upon which a family may be brought up with great advantage. We English, as a nation, think too much of persons, and too little of *things, work, execution*. Our children are allowed to make their figures or their letters, their stitches, their dolls' clothes, their small carpentry, anyhow, with the notion that they will do better by-and-by. Other nations—the Germans and the French, for instance—look at the question philosophically, and know that if children get the *habit* of turning out imperfect work, the men and women will undoubtedly keep that habit up. I remember being delighted with the work of a class of about forty children, of six and seven, in an elementary school at Heidelberg. They were doing a writing lesson, accompanied by a good deal of oral teaching from a master, who wrote each word on the blackboard. By-and-by the slates were shown, and I did not observe *one faulty or irregular letter* on the whole forty slates. The same principle of 'perfection' was to be discerned in a recent exhibition of schoolwork held throughout France. No faulty work was shown, to be excused on the plea that it was the work of children" (Vol. 1, pp. 159, 160).

14. Give your child good copies to imitate.

"Set good copies before him, and see that he imitates his model dutifully" (Vol. 1, p. 234).

15. Have your child evaluate his writing compared to the model and have him point out what is wrong.

"Set him six strokes to copy; let him, not bring a slateful, but six perfect strokes, at regular distances and at regular slopes. If he produces a faulty pair, get *him* to point out the fault, and persevere until he has produced his task" (Vol. 1, p. 160).

16. Set a goal for your child of producing a few perfect letters or a single line copied exactly. When he reaches the goal, the lesson is done.

"His writing task is to produce six perfect *m*'s: he writes six lines with only one good *m* in each line; the time for the writing lesson is over and he has none for himself; or, he is able to point out six good *m*'s in his first line, and he has the rest of the time to draw steamboats and railway trains" (Vol. 1, p. 143).

"The writing lesson being, not so many lines, or 'a copy'—that is, a page of

Notes

"Let the child accomplish something perfectly in every lesson—a stroke, a pothook, a letter."

writing—but a single line which is as exactly as possible a copy of the characters set. The child may have to write several lines before he succeeds in producing this" (Vol. 1, p. 235).

"If he does not do it to-day, let him go on to-morrow and the next day, and when the six perfect strokes appear, let it be an occasion of triumph" (Vol. 1, p. 160).

17. Teach printing before cursive, possibly italics style.

"But the child should have practice in printing before he begins to write" (Vol. 1, p. 234).

18. Teach capital letters before lowercase letters.

"First, let him print the simplest of the capital letters with single curves and straight lines. When he can make the capitals and large letters, with some firmness and decision, he might go on to the smaller letters" (Vol. 1, p. 234).

19. Your child should write simple, large letters for beginning writing lessons.

"When he can make the capitals and large letters, with some firmness and decision, he might go on to the smaller letters—'printed' as in the type we call 'italics,' only upright,—as simple as possible, and large" (Vol. 1, p. 234).

20. Writing lessons should group letters with similar strokes. Charlotte's students followed this sequence.

These letter groupings are based on the style of handwriting that Charlotte used for her students. You may need to reorganize which letters should be grouped together if you are using a different style.

1. Learn to draw a straight line.
2. Learn to draw a hooked line.
3. Learn to draw letters that are made up of a straight line and a hooked line: *n, m, v, w, r, h, p, y.*
4. Learn to draw a circle.
5. Learn to draw letters with a curve in them: *a, c, g, e, x, s, q.*
6. Learn looped and irregular letters: *b, l, f, t,* etc.

"Let the stroke be learned first; then the pothook; then the letters of which the pothook is an element—*n, m, v, w, r, h, p, y*; then *o*, and letters of which the curve is an element—*a, c, g, e, x, s, q*; then looped and irregular letters—*b, l, f, t,* etc." (Vol. 1, p. 234).

21. Writing lessons should follow this technique.

1. Day One: Form one letter perfectly.
2. Day Two: Form another letter that uses the same element.
3. Repeat until that element and its letters are familiar.
4. Form letters into words as soon as possible for the student to copy. The goal is to write the word once without a mistake.
5. Continue in this fashion with an emphasis on making perfect letters.

"If children get the habit of turning out imperfect work, the men and women will undoubtedly keep that habit up."

"One letter should be perfectly formed in a day, and the next day the same elemental forms repeated in another letter, until they become familiar. By-and-by copies, three or four of the letters they have learned grouped into a word—'man,' 'aunt'; the lesson to be the production of the written word *once* without a single fault in any letter" (Vol. 1, p. 234).

22. Do not hurry or pressure a child to have beautiful handwriting; that will come by and by.

"Of the further stages, little need be said. Secure that the child *begins* by making perfect letters and is never allowed to make faulty ones, and the rest he will do for himself; as for 'a good hand,' do not hurry him; his 'handwriting' will come by-and-by out of the character that is in him; but, as a child, he cannot be said, strictly speaking, to have character" (Vol. 1, p. 234).

"Secure that the child begins by making perfect letters and is never allowed to make faulty ones, and the rest he will do for himself."

Part 2

Handwriting Lessons

Capital Letters & Strokes

Supplies Needed

- Pan of raw rice or sand if desired
- Dry erase board with markers or chalkboard with chalk
- *Delightful Handwriting* Copybook (one for each child)
- Pencil

Charlotte wanted students to practice the elements of the alphabet before moving on to the actual letters: "Let the stroke be learned first; then the pothook; then the letters of which the pothook is an element . . . ."

We'll teach each new element before teaching the capitals that use those elements, starting with capital letters with straight lines, moving to capitals with single curves and straight lines, and finishing up with double curve capitals.

If your child is ready, feel free to skip the air- and pan-of-rice drawing and proceed directly to chalkboard and paper.

Lesson 1

Learn the stroke.

Zaner Bloser

D'Nealian

In the air, using your finger, make a simple line from top to bottom, the element called the stroke. (For the D'Nealian font, your stroke will be slanted with the top starting at the right and ending at the bottom with the stroke slightly to the left.) With your child sitting next to you, have him imitate you. He can also make a stroke in a pan of rice or sand. Have him pat out the image if it's not formed correctly and keep making it until he can make it flawlessly. Make a stroke on the chalkboard or dry erase board and have him copy the model, erasing as often as needed until he has a nice straight line. A short lesson in copywork that ends with success will give your child confidence and anticipation for the next lesson!

Lesson 2

1. Review and write the stroke.

Let your child make another perfect stroke on the chalkboard or dry erase board and once he is confident, he can make one in his copybook on page 3. Use any features of the copybook pages described below that will work best for your student. He might

- trace the large stroke in the box, using his finger;
- practice writing the stroke in the blank space beside the box, using a pencil;
- trace the smaller stroke with his finger, getting a "feel" for how it fits inside the guide lines;
- trace the smaller stroke with a pencil;
- practice writing the stroke inside the guide lines with a pencil. If he's not satisfied that it follows the model exactly, he can continue to make a careful stroke until he gets one perfect one.
- If you haven't used the blank space beside the box at the top of the page, you might allow your student to draw a picture there or place a sticker there after this step is accomplished.

When writing with pencil and paper, your child should be practicing good sitting positions with plenty of light to see by and correct pencil-holding procedures.

2. Learn the side stroke.

Zaner Bloser or D'Nealian

Once a perfect stroke is accomplished he can move on to the side stroke. This is simply a stroke starting from your left and ending at your right. With your child sitting next to you (instead of face to face with you, so he can see the element made in the correct direction), draw the side stroke in the air, allowing him to copy your movements. Move on to making a side stroke in a pan of rice or sand. And then draw a side stroke on the chalkboard or dry erase board and have him copy your model as exactly as possible, erasing to his heart's content until he makes a perfect one.

If your child is a very new beginning writer, he may not be ready to write in his copybook yet. The black board and chalk may be sufficient for him for now: "At this stage the chalk and blackboard are better than pen and paper, as it is well that the child should rub out and rub out until his own eye is satisfied with the word or letter he has written" (Vol. 1, p. 234).

Lesson 3

1. Review and write the side stroke.

Review the side stroke on the board, having your child make an exact copy of the model, and then draw a side stroke in his copybook on page 4 until he has made one perfect side stroke. You may use any of the features of the copybook page mentioned in Lesson 2 to help your student be successful.

The page in the copybook shows the side stroke in different locations on the guide lines. Help your child notice the various locations in preparation for learning capital *E*.

2. *Learn capital* E.

 Zaner Bloser    D'Nealian

And now for a letter! In the air, using your finger, follow the arrows to make the capital letter *E*. Make it big and have your child sitting beside you so that he can see the correct direction. He can then draw a big *E* in the air with starts and stops correctly made.

Next have him make *E* with his finger in a pan of rice. If it is wobbly or unclear, have him immediately pat it out and make a better one.

Lastly, write *E* for him on the chalkboard or dry erase board. Then have your child make one perfect capital *E*, erasing as often as needed until he is satisfied that it looks like the model.

"Set good copies before him, and see that he imitates his model dutifully: the writing lesson being, not so many lines, or 'a copy'—that is, a page of writing—but a single line which is as exactly as possible a copy of the characters set. The child may have to write several lines before he succeeds in producing this" (Vol. 1, p. 235).

Lesson 4

1. *Review and write* E.

Have your child draw capital *E* on the board. Once he is confident in his work, let him make a good *E* in his copybook on page 5. If it is not satisfactory, let him continue to make capital *E* carefully until a perfect one is attained.

Use the tracing and practice features of the copybook page as needed for your child to be successful. Be watchful that he is not slipshod in his work until a good *E* just happens to be printed. "Secure that the child *begins* by making perfect letters and is never allowed to make faulty ones . . . ." (Vol. 1, p. 234).

2. Learn capital F.

Zaner Bloser   D'Nealian

Once *E* is reviewed, move on to making capital *F*. If helpful, depending on the level of your child, make *F* with your finger in the air followed by your child copying your motions. Have him make *F* in a pan of rice, wiping out any incorrectly formed *F*'s until a perfect one is made. Then proceed to the chalkboard or dry erase board. Demonstrate a good model *F* and have him make one perfect capital *F*, erasing and redoing as often as needed until an excellent *F* is produced.

Lesson 5

1. Review and write capital F.

Review capital *F* on the board with your child making an exact *F*. When he knows he can do it well, have him make a good *F* in his copybook on page 6.

2. Learn capital H.

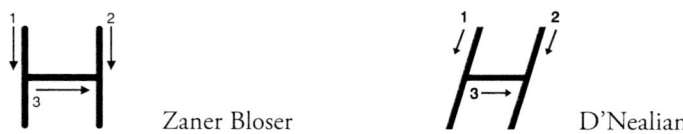

Zaner Bloser   D'Nealian

With your child sitting beside you, follow the arrows to draw an *H* in the air for your child to copy with his finger. Follow air-writing with making an *H* in the pan of rice. And then make a good capital *H* on the board for your child to copy. Let his eye be trained to recognize when he needs to erase and continue trying for a perfect *H*: ". . . it is well that the child should rub out and rub out until his own eye is satisfied with the word or letter he has written" (Vol. 1, p. 234).

Lesson 6

1. *Review and write capital* H.

Let your child review capital *H* on the board, and if he is ready for pencil and paper, he can write *H* in his copybook on page 7.

Once he can write *H* satisfactorily, he is ready to combine letters he knows to write a word. Have him write the word *HE* until his eye is satisfied that both letters in the word are exactly like the model in his copybook.

2. *Learn capital* I.

Zaner Bloser   D'Nealian

Capital *I* is the next letter to be learned. Draw it in the air with your child. Have him practice it in his pan of rice. Then write a good capital *I* on the board and let your child make an *I*, erasing until an accurate one is achieved.

Writing is hard work for new learners, so right now accuracy is what you want to see. Writing will become easier with practice once he has secured the habit of excellent work.

"Ease in writing comes by practice; but that must be secured later. In the meantime, the thing to be avoided is the habit of careless work—humpy m's, angular o's" (Vol. 1, p. 234).

Notes

Lesson 7

1. *Review and write capital* I.

Review capital *I* on the board, and when your child is confident, he can write *I* in his copybook on page 8. He should also be ready to write the word *IF* in nice letters in his copybook.

2. *Learn capital* L.

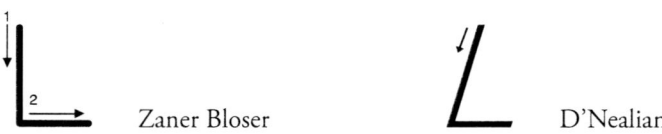

Zaner Bloser   D'Nealian

Work with your child to air-write capital *L* and draw *L* in a pan of rice. Then make a good *L* on the board for him to copy with chalk or dry erase marker until he has it perfect.

Spend several days on review pages if necessary. Your child may be able to write only one perfect word per day.

Lesson 8

Review letters by copying words.

Now your child can review the letters he has learned by copying the words *HI* and *FEE* on page 9 of the copybook. Take your time and emphasize good work more than speed. Encourage him to make an exact copy of each word before moving on.

If your child is using *Delightful Reading*, the words on the review pages for the capital letters will give him another opportunity to read words he has learned in the lessons on *Rain* by Robert Louis Stevenson.

Lesson 9

1. Review and write capital L.

Review *L* on the board and on page 10 of the copybook, and then your child can move on to making a good copy of the word *LIFE* in his copybook. Have him write it until he gets a correct copy of the word. If he cannot get it exact in 5–10 minutes, put away his copywork until tomorrow when he can freshly try again.

"If he produces a faulty pair, get him to point out the fault, and persevere until he has produced his task; if he does not do it to-day, let him go on to-morrow and the next day, and when six perfect strokes appear, let it be an occasion of triumph" (Vol. 1, p. 160).

2. Learn capital T.

Zaner Bloser   D'Nealian

Use air-writing and a pan of rice to teach capital *T,* and then let your child copy your good example on the board, rubbing out until his eye is satisfied with an exact copy of capital *T.*

Lesson 10

1. Review and write capital T.

Review capital *T* on the board, then have your child write capital *T* and the word *THE* in his copybook on page 11.

2. Learn the forward slash.

Zaner Bloser or D'Nealian

We're ready to learn some new elements for our capital letters. (If you are using the D'Nealian font, notice how the forward slash is slightly more slanted than the basic stroke learned in Lesson 1.)

With your child sitting beside you, draw a slanted stroke in the air from top to bottom starting at the right and ending at the left: /. Let him copy your motions with his finger in the air, and then let him draw a slanted stroke, or forward slash, in his pan of rice. Lastly, he can copy your good example on the board.

Lesson 11

1. Review and write the forward slash.

Review the forward slash stroke on the board and then your child can produce one or two or up to six (depending on what you think your child is capable of) good slanted strokes in his copybook on page 12.

2. Learn the back slash.

Zaner Bloser

D'Nealian

And now the back slash will be learned. Draw with your finger in the air a slanted line from top to bottom starting at the left and ending at the right: \. Have your child also make one in a pan of rice and then copy your example on the board, erasing and redoing until he has a perfect backward slanted stroke.

Lesson 12

1. Review and write the back slash.

Review the back slash on the board, and have your child make as many copies of the back slash in his copybook on page 13 as he needs to until one or two or up to six perfect strokes are completed.

2. Learn capital A.

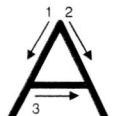 Zaner Bloser   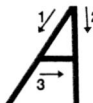 D'Nealian

Capital *A* will be learned today. Air-write and use a pan of rice to teach *A* if you feel those methods are a helpful start for your child. Then have your child imitate your model *A* on the board until he successfully makes a perfect capital *A*.

Lesson 13

1. Review and write capital A.

Review *A* on the board. When your child is confident he can make a perfect one, let him write capital *A* and the word *ALL* in his copybook on page 14 as many times as he needs to until he gets a good copy with all letters perfect. Let him notice if he needs to continue. And remember to make it an occasion of triumph when he does get a perfect copy!

(D'Nealian) 1b. Learn the pothook stroke.

Teach your child a pothook today. This element is a little mark or tail at the end of some of the D'Nealian-style letters. (See the example on the *K* below.) Demonstrate with air-writing, a pan of rice, and on the board. Let your child practice until a good copy is achieved.

2. Learn capital K.

"First, let the child accomplish something perfectly in every lesson—a stroke, a pothook, a letter" (Vol. 1, p. 233).

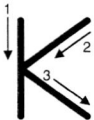 Zaner Bloser   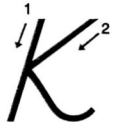 D'Nealian

Teach capital *K* with air-writing, a pan of rice, and on the board, letting your child complete a perfect *K*.

Lesson 14

1. Review and write capital **K.**

Let your child review *K* on the board, and then write it along with the word *KIT* in his copybook on page 15.

2. Learn capital **M.**

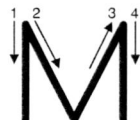 Zaner Bloser    D'Nealian

Teach capital *M* with air-writing, a pan of rice, and finally, on the board with your child finishing an excellent *M*.

"Not more than ten minutes or a quarter of an hour should be given to the early writing-lessons" (Vol. 1, p. 239).

Lesson 15

1. Review and write capital **M.**

Review *M* on the board. When ready, have your child write capital *M* and the word *MAT* perfectly in his copybook on page 16.

2. Learn capital **N.**

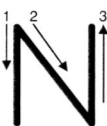 Zaner Bloser    D'Nealian

Teach capital *N* with air-writing, a pan of rice, and the board. Celebrate when excellent work is accomplished! And if needed, leave off the lesson at 5–10 minutes and continue it tomorrow with renewed vigor.

Spend several days on review pages if necessary. Your child may be able to write only one perfect word per day.

Lesson 16

Review letters by writing words.

Now your child can review the letters he has learned by copying the words *KIM, HIT,* and *FLEA* on pages 17 and 18 of the copybook. Use the extra lines on page 18 for more practice and review if desired.

Lesson 17

1. Review and write capital N.

Have your child make another perfect capital *N* on the board and then write a good copy of it and the word *MAIN* in his copybook on page 19.

2. Learn capital V.

 Zaner Bloser    D'Nealian

Capital *V* will be the new letter learned today. Use air-writing, a pan of rice, and the board to teach *V* to your child.

Lesson 18

1. Review and write capital V.

Review *V* on the board, letting your child make a perfect one. Then let him write capital *V* and the word *VAT* in his copybook on page 20.

2. Learn capital W.

Stop formal lessons and review trouble letters or elements for your daily lesson as often as needed. Then you can continue with new letters when your child is ready.

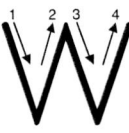 Zaner Bloser    D'Nealian

Capital *W* is next. Teach your child using air-writing, a pan of rice, and a good model on the board, letting him erase and redo *W* until his eye recognizes an excellent example.

Lesson 19

1. Review and write capital W.

Let your child review *W* on the board and write a good copy of it along with the word *WHAT* in his copybook on page 21.

2. Learn capital X.

Zaner Bloser

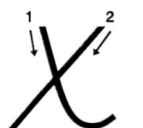
D'Nealian

Teach capital *X* using air-writing, a pan of rice and the board. (Notice for D'Nealian font that one of the lines has a little pothook at the bottom. Review that element as needed to accomplish a perfect copy.) Show excitement with the completion of good work!

Lesson 20

1. Review and write capital X.

Review capital *X* on the board until an impeccable *X* is attained. Have your child carefully write it and the word *EXIT* in his copybook on page 22.

2. Learn capital Y.

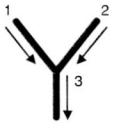
Zaner Bloser

D'Nealian

Follow the arrows to teach capital *Y* using air-writing and a pan of rice. Then let your child copy your model of *Y* on the board until a very good copy is made.

"By-and-by copies, three or four of the letters they have learned grouped into a word—'man,' 'aunt'; the lesson to be a production of the written word once *without a single fault in any letter"* (Vol. 1, p. 234).

Lesson 21

1. Review and write capital Y.

Have your child write capital *Y* on the board until he is confident he can make an excellent copy on paper. Then let him write *Y* and the word *YEA* in his copybook on page 23.

2. Learn capital Z.

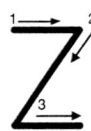 Zaner Bloser  D'Nealian

Teach capital *Z* using air-writing, a pan of rice, and your good model on the board. Let your child continue to erase and redo his *Z* on the board until he makes an excellent copy.

A timer is a good way to make sure you aren't doing too long of lessons for your child. It's also a visual clue for him to know that there is an end to the lesson, so he can give his very best effort for the full 10 or so minutes and not pick up the habit of dawdling.

Lesson 22

1. Review and write capital Z.

Review capital *Z* on the board, and then your child can write *Z* and the word *ZANY* in his copywork book on page 24.

2. Learn the C-curve.

 Zaner Bloser  D'Nealian

Today we move on to teaching a few more elements needed before finishing up capital letters. Demonstrate a large C-type curve in the air. (For the D'Nealian font, notice that the top will have a slight slant toward the right.) Have your child make it in his pan of rice. And then draw a good C-curve on the board for your child to copy.

Lesson 23

1. Review and write the C-curve.

Review the C-curve on the board with your child. Then let him make one or two or up to six good copies of this element in his copybook on page 25.

2. Learn the U-curve.

 Zaner Bloser    D'Nealian

Today you will teach another curve: one that is shaped like a lower case *u*. (This stroke is to help make the letters *J* and *U*.) Make a small u-shaped curve in the air and in a pan of rice and, lastly, on the board.

Lesson 24

Review letters by copying words.

Review letters your child has learned by letting him copy the words *WIT* and *YE* on page 26 of the copybook. Take your time and emphasize good work more than speed. Encourage him to make an exact copy of each word before moving on.

Lesson 25

Review letters by copying words.

Now your child can review more letters by copying the words *VAIN, ZAZZY,* and *NEXT* on pages 27 and 28 of the copybook. The extra lines on page 28 can be used for more practice as desired.

Be sure the desk or table is at a comfortable height for your child, that he uses correct pencil holding techniques, and that there is good lighting for him to see by.

Lesson 26

1. Review and write the U-curve.

Review the u-shaped curve on the board before your child moves on to making good copies in his copybook on page 29.

2. Learn the backward C-curve.

Zaner Bloser   D'Nealian

And now teach your child the backward C-shaped curve (D'Nealian font will have a slight slant to the right, a little like the right side of a heart shape.) using air-writing, a pan of rice, and the board. Let your child end the lesson with an excellent shape.

Lesson 27

1. Review and write the backward C-curve.

Review the backward C-shaped curve on the board and let your child make several perfect copies in his copybook on page 30.

2. Learn capital C.

Zaner Bloser   D'Nealian

You are now ready for more letters! Capital *C* will be learned today. Use air-writing, a pan of rice, and the board to teach it to your child, ending with an exact copy of your model on the board.

Lesson 28

1. Review and write capital C.

Let your child make a good copy of *C* on the board, and then let him write capital *C* and the word *CHAT* in his copybook on page 31.

2. *Learn capital* D.

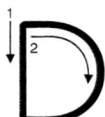 Zaner Bloser    D'Nealian

Teach capital *D* using air-writing, a pan of rice, and the board, celebrating excellently accomplished work!

Lesson 29

1. *Review and write capital* D.

Review *D* on the board, then let your child make a good copy of it, plus the word *WIELD*, in his copybook on page 32.

2. *Learn capital* G.

 Zaner Bloser    D'Nealian

Teach capital *G* with air-writing, a pan of rice, and a copy of your good model on the board.

Lesson 30

1. *Review and write capital* G.

Review *G* on the board and let your child make a good copy of it and the word *AGAIN* in his copybook on page 33.

2. *Learn capital* J.

Let your child continue to train his eye and to point out any faults in his letters and words as he strives to make exact copies.

Notes

Use air-writing, a pan of rice, and the board to teach capital *J* to your child, getting him to point out when he needs to erase and redo his copy on the board.

Lesson 31

1. Review and write capital J.

Capital *J* can be reviewed with the board and by your child perfecting a *J* and a copy of the word *JACK* in his copybook on page 34.

2. Learn capital O.

Teach capital *O* today using air-writing, a pan of rice, and the board.

Lesson 32

1. Review and write capital O.

Have your child make a perfect copy of the letter *O* on the board before he writes *O* and the word *WON* in his copybook on page 35.

2. Learn capital P.

Teach capital *P* using air-writing, a pan of rice, and a good copy on the board.

Lesson 33

Review letters by copying words.

Review more letters that your child has learned. Have him copy the words *CAT, JON,* and *GLAND* on pages 36 and 37 of the copybook. Be careful not to rush him, but encourage him to make an exact copy of each word before moving on. Use the extra lines on page 37 for more practice if desired.

"Set good copies before him, and see that he imitates his model dutifully" (Vol. 1, p. 23).

Lesson 34

1. Review and write capital P.

Review *P* on the board and let your child write a good copy of it and the word *DIP* in his copybook on page 38.

2. Learn capital Q.

 Zaner Bloser    D'Nealian

Teach capital *Q* with air-writing, rice, and an excellent model to follow on the board.

Lesson 35

1. Review and write capital Q.

Review *Q* on the board with your child and let him practice writing the letter in his copybook on page 39.

2. Learn capital R.

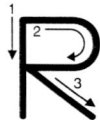 Zaner Bloser    D'Nealian

Teach capital *R* next using air-writing, rice, and a final perfect copy of the letter on the board. (Notice for D'Nealian style that the line curves with a pothook element. Practice this element first if your child needs the extra attention in this area.)

Lesson 36

1. Review and write capital R.

Review *R* on the board and let your child write a perfect copy of that letter along with the word *MERE* in his copybook on page 40.

2. Learn capital U.

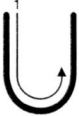 Zaner Bloser    D'Nealian

Teach capital *U* today using air-writing and a pan of rice if helpful for your young writer. (Notice that the D'Nealian font has an extra "tail" or pothook.) When he has grasped the shape, he can practice making a perfect *U* on the board.

Lesson 37

1. Review and write capital U.

Review *U* on the board and then your child can write a good copy of it and the word *QUIT* in his copybook on page 41.

2. Learn capital **B.**

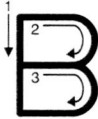 Zaner Bloser    D'Nealian

Use air-writing, a pan of rice, and copies on the board to teach the capital letter *B*. Large letters are best for early writers.

Lesson 38

1. *Review and write capital* **B.**

Review *B* on the board, being sure your child ends the review with an excellent copy. Then he can write one, along with the word *BOUND,* in his copybook on page 42.

2. *Learn capital* **S.**

 Zaner Bloser    D'Nealian

Today is your last capital letter to be taught! Teach capital *S* by drawing in the air; then let your child make a good copy in a pan of rice. And lastly, let him draw a good copy from your model on the board. Celebrate success!

"When he can make the capitals and large letters, with some firmness and decision, he might go on to the small letters—'printed' as in the type we call 'italics', only upright,— as simple as possible, and large" (Vol. 1, p. 234).

Lesson 39

Review and write capital **S.**

Review capital *S* on the board. When an excellent *S* is attained, let your child write it along with the word *SKIPS* in his copybook on page 43.

Lesson 40

Review letters by copying words.

Notes

Review more capital letters your child has learned by having him copy the words *QUIPS* and *BRAND* on page 44 of the copybook.

Lesson 41

My Name Is.

On page 45 in the copybook your child may write his name using the capital letters he has learned. You may decide whether you want him to also copy the words already on the page, *MY NAME IS.*

However you choose to use the page, make sure you celebrate your child's success in learning all the capital letters and whet his appetite to go on to the lowercase letters next.

Lowercase Letters & Strokes

Following Charlotte's principles, now that your child has learned the simpler capital letters, we will move on to the lowercase letters. We'll teach those letters that use the stroke first, then those that have the element of a curve. We won't be following Charlotte's suggested order exactly, because the font she was describing is different from our own.

Remember

~ Short lessons. Pay attention to your child's cues. If he's frustrated, shorten the lesson. You want to end a lesson with your child wanting more.

~ Large print with accuracy being the goal. Ease will come with practice.

~ Skip the air-writing and pan-of-rice practice if needed. Use only chalkboard and chalk or dry erase board and markers if your child is not ready to write with pencil and paper. You can always come back and try pencil and paper in a few months.

~ Let the child's eye be trained to recognize good work versus slipshod work. Allow him to point out when his letters and words do not match the model.

~ Stop and review/practice faulty letters as often as needed.

~ Be sure lighting is good and that pencil grip and desk height are correct.

~ Many lowercase letters are similar to their uppercase forms, but those similarities may vary according to what font you use. In a couple of instances, the D'Nealian and Zaner Bloser fonts will need to be approached differently. When that happens, the lessons are labeled separately; simply follow your chosen style of font.

Lesson 42

Review and write the basic strokes.

Since the basic elements have been learned already, use today's lesson for reviewing and practicing the stroke elements a little smaller (lowercase letter size) in the copybook on page 46.

Zaner Bloser   D'Nealian

Lesson 43

Review and write lowercase v.

Explain that lowercase *v* is written just like capital *V* only smaller. Have your child review *v* by making a very good copy on the board. When his eye is satisfied that he has made a good one, let him write a perfect *v* in his copybook on page 47. If the first one is not perfect, let him carefully keep trying until he makes one.

Lesson 44

1. Review and write lowercase z.

Let your child review *z* on the board, then he can produce one or two or up to six excellent copies of the smaller lowercase letter in his copybook on page 48.

2. Learn lowercase i.

Zaner Bloser   D'Nealian

Demonstrate lowercase *i* in the air and in a pan of rice. Then let him copy a very good *i* on the board. (Notice that the D'Nealian font has a pothook element.)

Lesson 45

1. Review and write lowercase i.

Review *i* on the board, and then your child can make a series of perfect *i*'s in his copybook on page 49. Show joy at his perseverance and accomplishment! If it takes the full amount of time to finish a letter review, then happily teach a new letter tomorrow.

2. Learn lowercase l.

Zaner Bloser   D'Nealian

Use air-writing and a pan of rice to teach lowercase *l*. Make a good model of *l* on the board and let your child do his very best to copy it perfectly, erasing and redoing as often as he needs to.

Lesson 46

Review letters.

Review the lowercase letters your child has learned by having him copy *i*, *v*, and *z* carefully on pages 50 and 51 of the copybook. Encourage him to do his best work and make one, two, or up to six exact copies of each letter before moving on. Use the extra lines on page 51 for other practice if desired.

Notes

"His writing task is to produce six perfect m*'s: he writes six lines with only one good* m *in each line; the time for the writing lesson is over and he has none for himself; or, he is able to point out six good* m*'s in his first line, and he has the rest of the time to draw steamboats and railway trains"* (Vol. 1, p. 143).

Lesson 47

1. Review and write lowercase l.

Let your child review *l* on the board until he is confident he can make an excellent one, then he can write an exact copy of *l* and the word *ill* in his copybook on page 52. Let him write the word until every letter matches the model, and triumph in successful completion!

2. Learn lowercase t.

Zaner Bloser   D'Nealian

Teach lowercase *t* using your finger in the air, and encourage your child to make a good *t* in a pan of rice. Finally, he can make a good *t* on the board.

Lesson 48

Review and write lowercase t.

Review *t* on the board and then your child can write *t* and the word *till* in his copybook on page 53.

Lesson 49

1. Review and write lowercase x.

Zaner Bloser   D'Nealian

Your child can review *x* by making a good copy of the letter on the board and then a series of good copies of the lowercase letter in his copybook on page 54. Let him know that lowercase *x* is just like capital *X* only smaller.

1b. Optional D'Nealian review element.

If you are using the D'Nealian font, you can review a lowercase u-curve and backward c-curve if needed. The next three letters of this font involve a curve element.

2. Learn lowercase k.

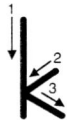 Zaner Bloser    D'Nealian

Teach *k* using air-writing, a pan of rice, and the board. This letter can be tricky in any font, but especially spend time perfecting lower case *k* if you are using the D'Nealian style. It will be good practice for the upcoming letters as well.

Lesson 50

1. Review and write lowercase k.

Review the letter *k* by having your child write it on the board, erasing and rewriting until it is an excellent copy. Then he can write it and the word *kilt* in his copybook on page 55.

(D'Nealian) *2. Learn lowercase* w.

 D'Nealian

The Zaner Bloser lowercase *w* is the same as its capital *W*, so the lowercase does not need to be taught today if you are using that font style. However, the D'Nealian font's lowercase *w* is different. If you are using D'Nealian, you will want to teach lowercase *w* now.

Teach lowercase *w* using your finger in the air, a pan of rice, and finally the board. Let your child's eye notice when a pleasing and exact *w* has been made.

Notes

"In all writing lessons, free use should be made of the blackboard by both teacher and children by way of model and practice" (Vol. 1, p. 239).

Lesson 51

Review letters by writing words.

Review the lowercase letters your child has learned by having him copy *kit, Liz,* and *x* carefully on page 56 of his copybook. Let him take his time and try to imitate the good letter and word models well.

Lesson 52

1. Review and write lowercase w.

 Zaner Bloser    D'Nealian

On the board, let your child review *w*, then he may write a good copy of *w* and the word *kiwi* in his copybook on page 57.

2. Learn lowercase y.

 Zaner Bloser   D'Nealian

Lowercase *y* will be learned today. Let your child follow your instructions and make a good *y* in the air and in a pan of rice. Draw a good model of the letter on the board and your child can copy it, erasing as often as needed until a good copy is attained.

Lesson 53

Review and write lowercase y.

Let your child review *y* on the board, after which he can write it plus *xyz* in his copybook on page 58. Let him achieve excellent copies of all three letters.

Lesson 54

1. Review and write lowercase o.

 Zaner Bloser   D'Nealian

Review *o* on the board and explain that lowercase *o* is the same as capital *O*, just smaller. Let your child write it and the word *vow* in his copybook on page 59. The remaining letters will have curve elements, so make sure your child is comfortable making those smaller curves used in *o*.

2. Learn lowercase a.

 Zaner Bloser   D'Nealian

Follow the direction of the arrows to teach your child lowercase *a*, using air-writing, a pan of rice, and your good model on the board. Let him end by making an excellent copy of *a*.

"A child must first learn to control his hand and constrain it to obey his eye" (Vol. 1, p. 236).

Lesson 55

Review and write lowercase a.

Review *a* on the board. When your child is confident that he has made a perfect *a*, he can write it and the word *law* in his copybook on page 60.

Lesson 56

Review letters by writing words.

Review more lowercase letters your child has learned by having him copy *tot, yay,* and *wow* carefully on pages 61 and 62 of his copybook. Encourage him to do his best and make exact copies. Use the extra lines on page 62 for more practice if desired.

If your child is using *Delightful Reading*, the words on the review pages for the lowercase letters will give him another opportunity to read words he has learned in the lessons on *The Dogs and the Fox* and Proverbs 23:4 and 5.

Lesson 57

1. Review and write lowercase c.

 Zaner Bloser　　　　　 D'Nealian

Review *c* on the board and explain that lowercase *c* is similar to uppercase C. Then have your child write a good copy of lowercase *c* and the word *click* in his copybook on page 63.

2. Learn lowercase g.

 Zaner Bloser　　　　　 D'Nealian

Using your finger in the air and in a pan of rice, teach lowercase *g* today. Let your child make a perfect copy of your model on the board.

Lesson 58

1. Review and write lowercase g.

Review *g* on the board. Let your child write a lowercase *g* and the word *go* in his copybook on page 64.

2. Learn lowercase e.

 Zaner Bloser　　　　　 D'Nealian

Teach lowercase *e* using air-writing, a pan of rice, and the board, letting your child end with an excellent copy of *e*.

Lesson 59

Review and write lowercase e.

Your child can make another good copy of *e* on the board before writing it and the word *alive* in his copybook on page 65.

Lesson 60

1. Review and write lowercase s.

 Zaner Bloser   D'Nealian

Review *s* on the board. Explain that lowercase *s* is written a little smaller than capital *S*. Let your child write a good copy of lowercase *s* and the word *last* in his copybook on page 66.

(Zaner Bloser) 2. Learn lowercase u.

 Zaner Bloser

The D'Nealian lowercase *u* is written like its capital *U*, so you will not need to teach it today if you are using D'Nealian font style. If you are using Zaner Bloser, you will want to teach lowercase *u* as described below.

Teach lowercase *u* following the arrow directions with your finger in the air, then your child's finger in a pan of rice, and finally with chalk on the chalkboard or markers on the dry erase board. Let your child end by making an excellent *u* of his very best effort.

Lesson 61

Review letters by writing words.

Review more lowercase letters by letting your child copy *cast* and *eagle*

Notes

on page 67 of his copybook. Allow him to take as much time as he needs to carefully make an exact copy of each letter and word.

Lesson 62

1. Review and write lowercase u.

 Zaner Bloser   *u* D'Nealian

Review *u* on the board before your child writes it along with the word *you* in his copybook on page 68.

2. Learn lowercase q.

 Zaner Bloser   *q* D'Nealian

Teach lowercase *q* with air-writing, a pan of rice, and the board.

Lesson 63

1. Review and write lowercase q.

Review *q* on the board, and then your child can write it with the word *quick* in his copybook on page 69.

2. Learn lowercase b.

 Zaner Bloser   D'Nealian

Teach lowercase *b,* paying attention to arrow directions as you trace *b* in the air, in a pan of rice, and finally using chalk and chalkboard or markers and dry erase board.

Notes

"One word more; do not hurry the child into 'small hand'; . . . It is much easier for the child to get into an irregular scribble by way of 'small-hand,' than to get out of it again. In this, as in everything else, the care of the educator must be given, not only to the formation of good, but to the prevention of bad habits" (Vol. 1, p. 235).

Lesson 64

1. Review and write lowercase b.

Review *b* on the board, letting your child copy the letter as many times as necessary until he gets a very good *b*. Then let him write it with the word *box* in his copybook on page 70.

2. Learn lowercase h.

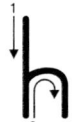 Zaner Bloser    D'Nealian

Teach *h* using air-writing, a pan of rice, and your good model on the board.

Lesson 65

1. Review and write lowercase h.

Review *h* on the board, then let your child write it with the word *shout* in his copybook on page 71.

2. Learn lowercase r.

 Zaner Bloser   D'Nealian

Teach lowercase *r* today using air-writing, a pan of rice, and the board.

Lesson 66

Review letters by writing words.

Review more lowercase letters your child has learned by having him carefully copy the words *quill, shut,* and *bog* on pages 72 and 73 of his copybook. Use the extra lines on page 73 for more practice if desired.

Lesson 67

1. Review and write lowercase r.

Your child can make a good copy of *r* on the board for review, and then he can write it with the word *hear* in his copybook on page 74.

2. Learn lowercase n.

 Zaner Bloser   D'Nealian

Lowercase *n* is the next letter to be taught with air-writing, a pan of rice, and the board.

Lesson 68

1. Review and write lowercase n.

Review *n* on the board before your child writes it and the word *brings* in his copybook on page 75 with every letter in the word being an excellent one.

2. Learn lowercase m.

 Zaner Bloser    D'Nealian

Teach lowercase *m* using air-writing, a pan of rice, and the board.

Lesson 69

1. Review and write lowercase **m.**

Review *m* on the board, then let your child write it along with the word *mare* in his copybook on page 76.

2. Learn lowercase **d.**

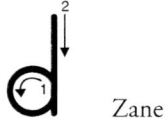 Zaner Bloser    D'Nealian

Pay attention to arrow directions as you teach lowercase *d* by drawing a large one in the air and letting your child copy you. Then let him draw one in a pan of rice being careful not to confuse *b* and *d*. He can then copy your model on the board.

Lesson 70

1. Review and write lowercase **d.**

Review *d* on the board and let your child write it with the word *grind* in his copybook on page 77.

2. Learn lowercase **j.**

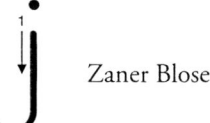 Zaner Bloser   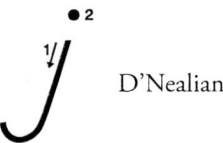 D'Nealian

Teach lowercase *j* using air-writing, a pan of rice, and the board.

Lesson 71

Review letters by writing words.

Review more lowercase letters by having your child copy *skin, dry,* and

"I should say that variety and beauty of form are attractive, even to little children, and that the attempt to create something which interests them, cheers and crowns their stupendous efforts with a pleasure that cannot be looked for in the task of copying monotonous shapes" (Vol. 1, p. 237).

home on pages 78 and 79 of his copybook. Let him take his time and try to imitate the good word models well. Use the extra lines on page 79 for more practice if desired.

Lesson 72

1. Review and write lowercase j.

Let your child review *j* on the board before writing it and the word *jaws* in his copybook on page 80.

2. Learn lowercase p.

Teach lowercase *p* today using air-writing, a pan of rice, and the board. Allow your child to end the lesson with an excellent example of *p* written on the board.

Lesson 73

1. Review and write lowercase p.

Review *p* on the board and then your child can write it with the word *paint* in his copybook on page 81.

2. Learn lowercase f.

Teach lowercase *f* using air-writing, a pan of rice, and the board. Celebrate good work done and the last letter of the alphabet to be learned!

Lesson 74

Review and write lowercase f.

Review *f* on the board and let your child write it with the word *doff* in his copybook on page 82.

Lesson 75

Review letters by writing words.

More review words are provided on pages 83 and 84 of the copybook. Let your child carefully copy *phone, finding,* and *jet,* taking his time and putting forth his best effort. Use the extra lines on page 84 to write more words that your child may want to copy. Now that he has learned all the letters, the possibilities are endless!

Lesson 76

Write your name.

Your child can again write his name, in capitals and lowercase letters this time, on page 85 in his copybook. He may write his first name only, or if able, he can write his middle and last name also.

Part 3

Copywork Selections

Copywork Selections

In the next section of your child's copybook, the text from the poem *Rain* by Robert Louis Stevenson, from *The Dogs and the Fox* by Aesop, and from Proverbs 23:4 and 5 are written out in large print for your child to copy.

In this teacher's book these reading selections have been divided into short suggested lessons. You may do one lesson a day by simply letting your child copy the words for that lesson in his copybook. Or if your child is ready to write more than a couple words a day, let him follow his own comfortable pace.

There will be some punctuation for your child to copy. Be sure to point out to your child when he'll be making a period or comma, etc. You might give a simple explanation of the role each mark plays at the time he comes upon it. Remember to keep the explanation very simple; your child will be encountering punctuation as he reads more and more, and he'll pick up each mark's meaning intuitively.

Keep lessons short, paying attention to your child's cues. Two words may be plenty, or he may be ready for much more than that. It's best to end a lesson with him in happy spirits instead of pushing him to his limit. You also want him to be giving his very best concentrated effort with each letter and word.

Rain
by Robert Louis Stevenson
(pages 86–89)

Lesson 77: The rain

Lesson 78: is falling

Lesson 79: all around,

Lesson 80: It falls

Lesson 81: on field

Lesson 82: and tree,

Lesson 83: It rains

Lesson 84: on the

Lesson 85: umbrellas here,

Lesson 86: And on the

Lesson 87: ships at sea.

The Dogs and the Fox
by Aesop
(pages 90–97)

Lesson 88: Some dogs,

Lesson 89: finding the

Lesson 90: skin of a lion

Lesson 91: began to

Lesson 92: tear it in

Lesson 93: pieces with

Lesson 94: their teeth.

Lesson 95: A fox,

Lesson 96: seeing them,

Lesson 97: said: "If this

Lesson 98: lion were

Lesson 99: alive, you

Lesson 100: would soon

Lesson 101: find out

Lesson 102: that his

Lesson 103: claws were

Lesson 104: stronger than

Lesson 105: your teeth."

Lesson 106: Moral: It is

Lesson 107: easy to kick

Lesson 108: a man that

Lesson 109: is down.

Proverbs 23:4 and 5
(pages 98–101)

Lesson 110: Do not wear

Lesson 111: yourself out to

Lesson 112: get rich; have

Lesson 113: the wisdom to

Lesson 114: show restraint.

Lesson 115: Cast but a

Lesson 116: glance at

Lesson 117: riches, and they

Lesson 118: are gone,

Lesson 119: for they will

Lesson 120: surely sprout

Lesson 121: wings and fly

Lesson 122: off to the sky

Lesson 123: like an eagle.

Zaner Bloser

Aa Bb Cc Dd Ee Ff

Gg Hh Ii Jj Kk Ll

Mm Nn Oo Pp Qq

Rr Ss Tt Uu Vv Ww

Xx Yy Zz

D'Nealian

Aa Bb Cc Dd Ee Ff Gg

Hh Ii Jj Kk Ll Mm Nn

Oo Pp Qq Rr Ss Tt Uu

Vv Ww Xx Yy Zz